It is a ...?

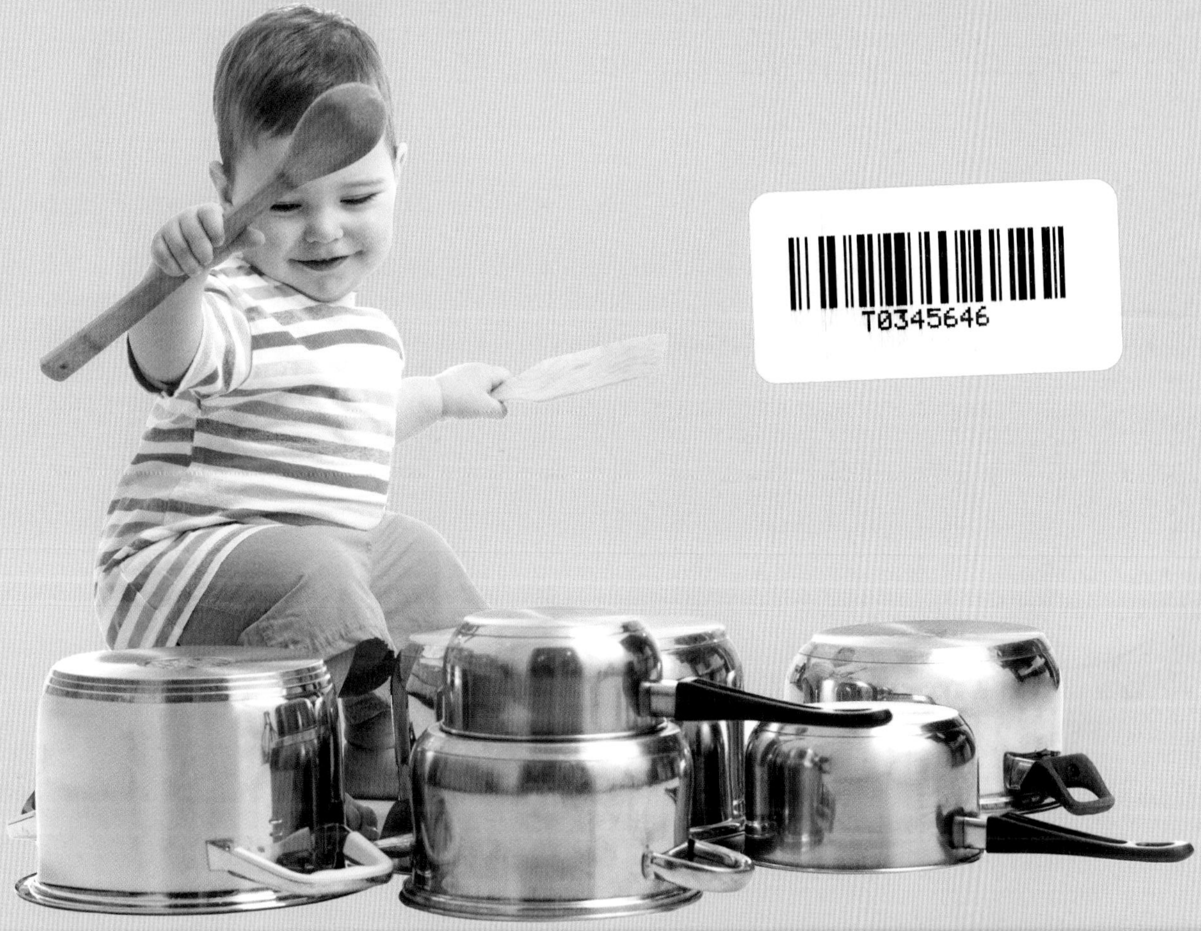

Written by Dominique Simpson

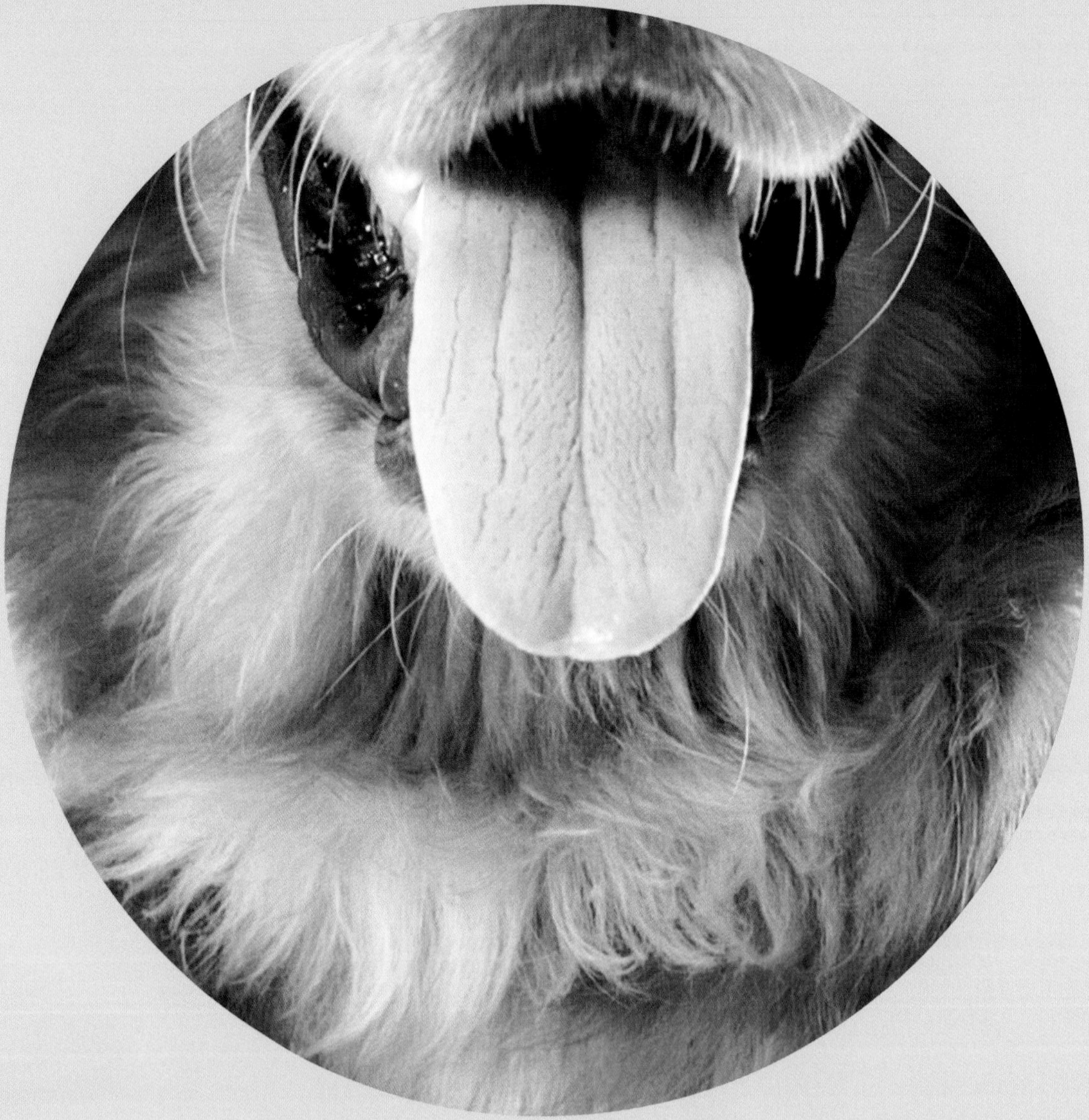

Is it a dog?

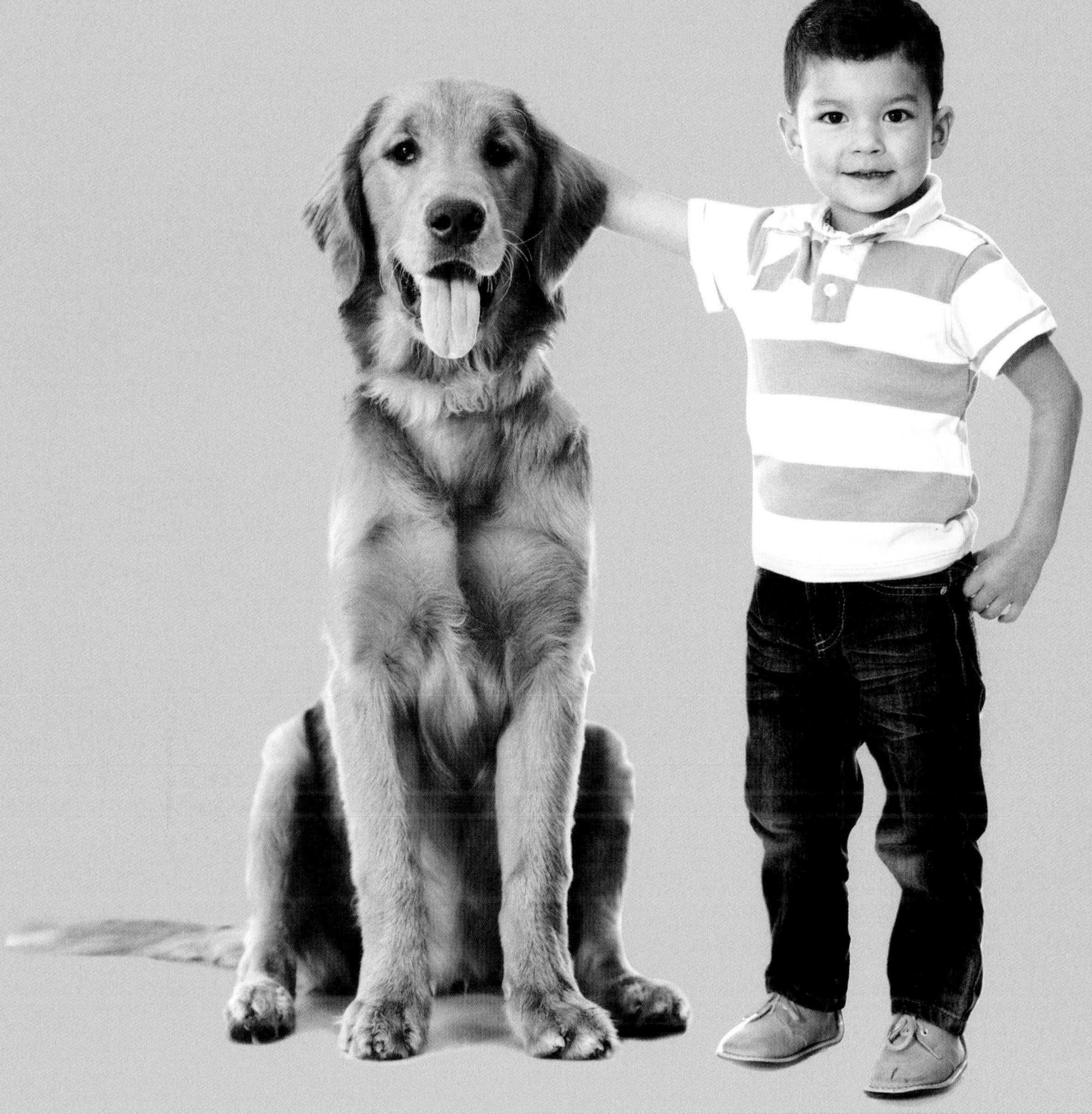

It is a dog to pat!

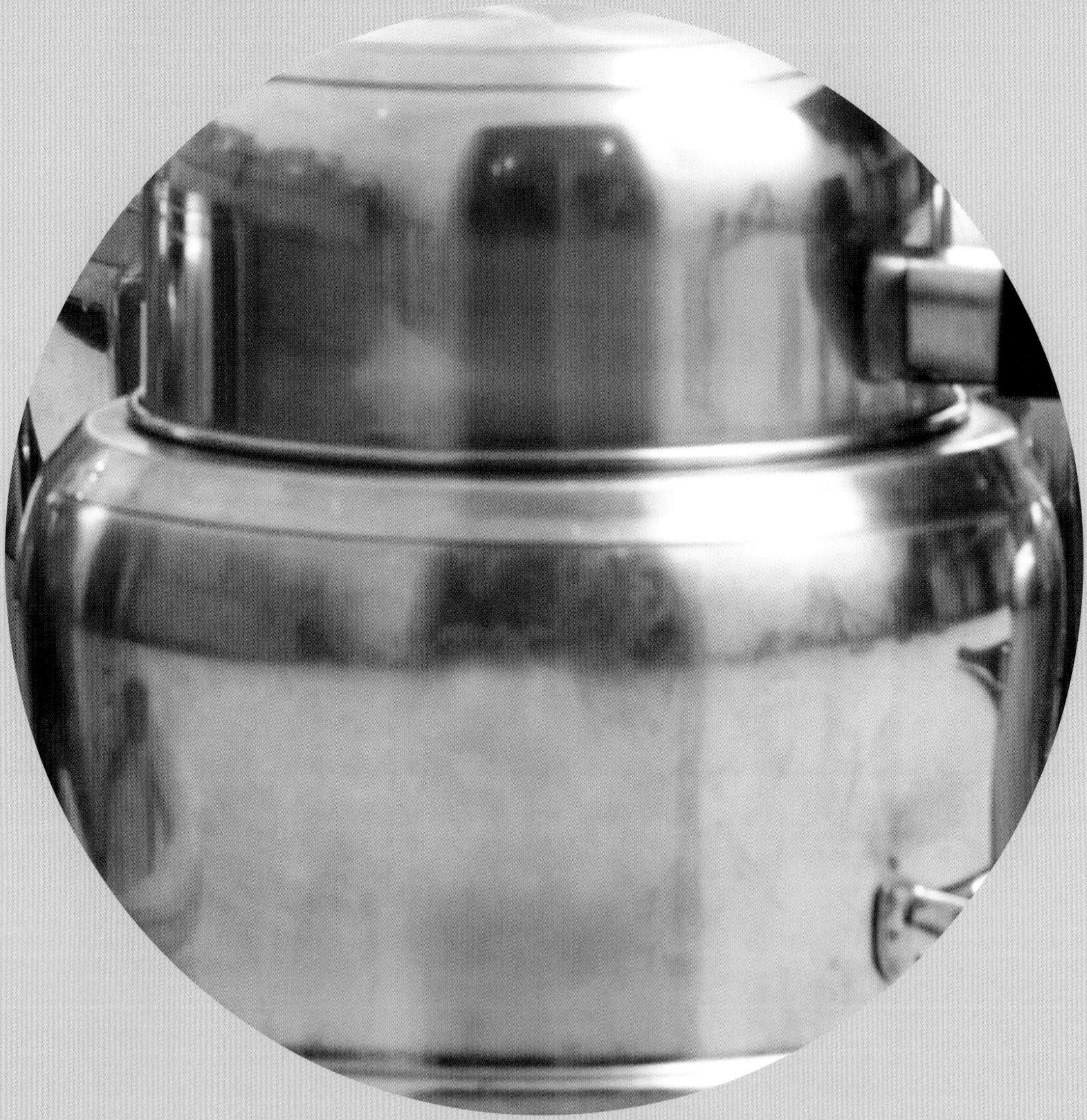

Is it a pan?

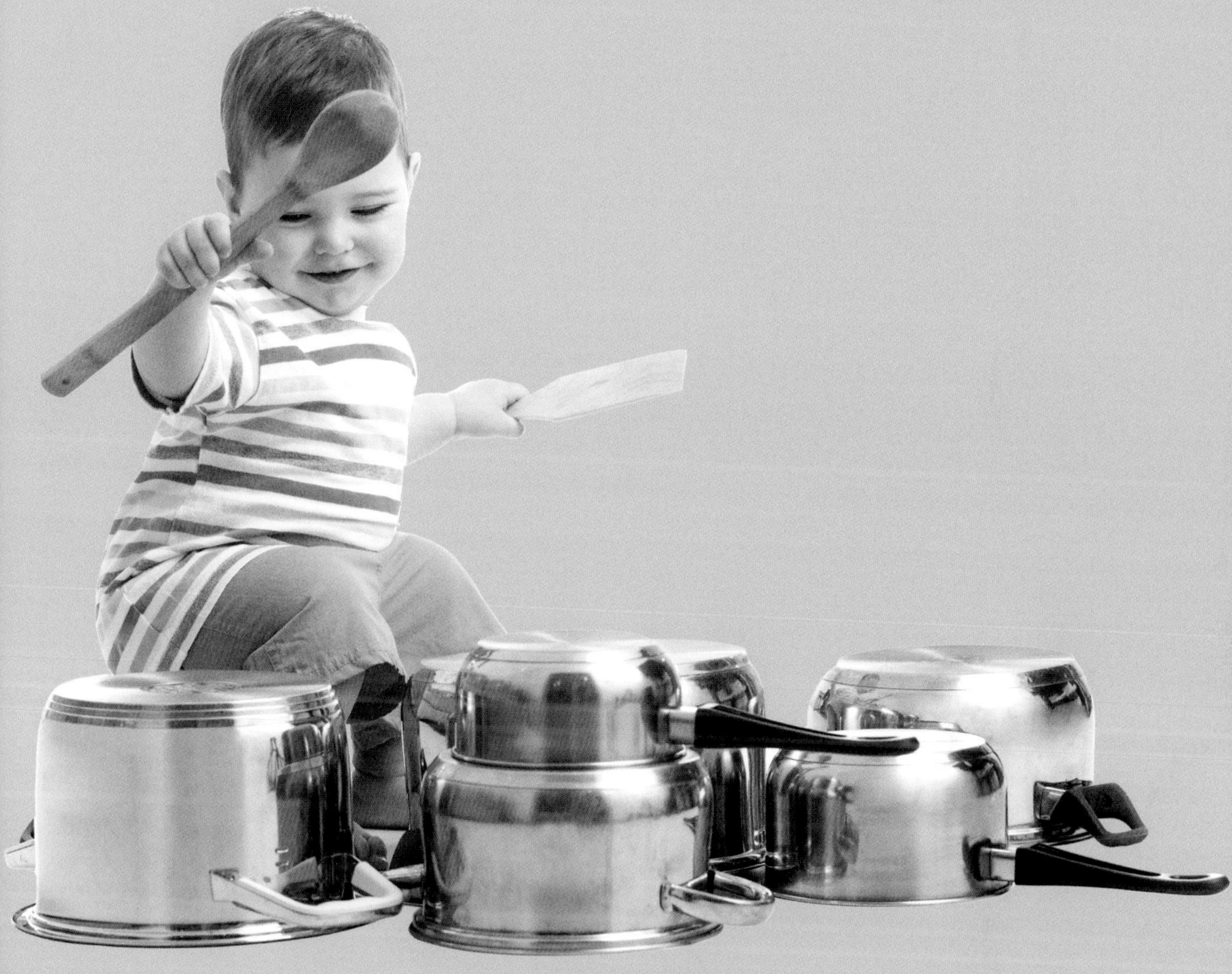

It is a pan to tap!

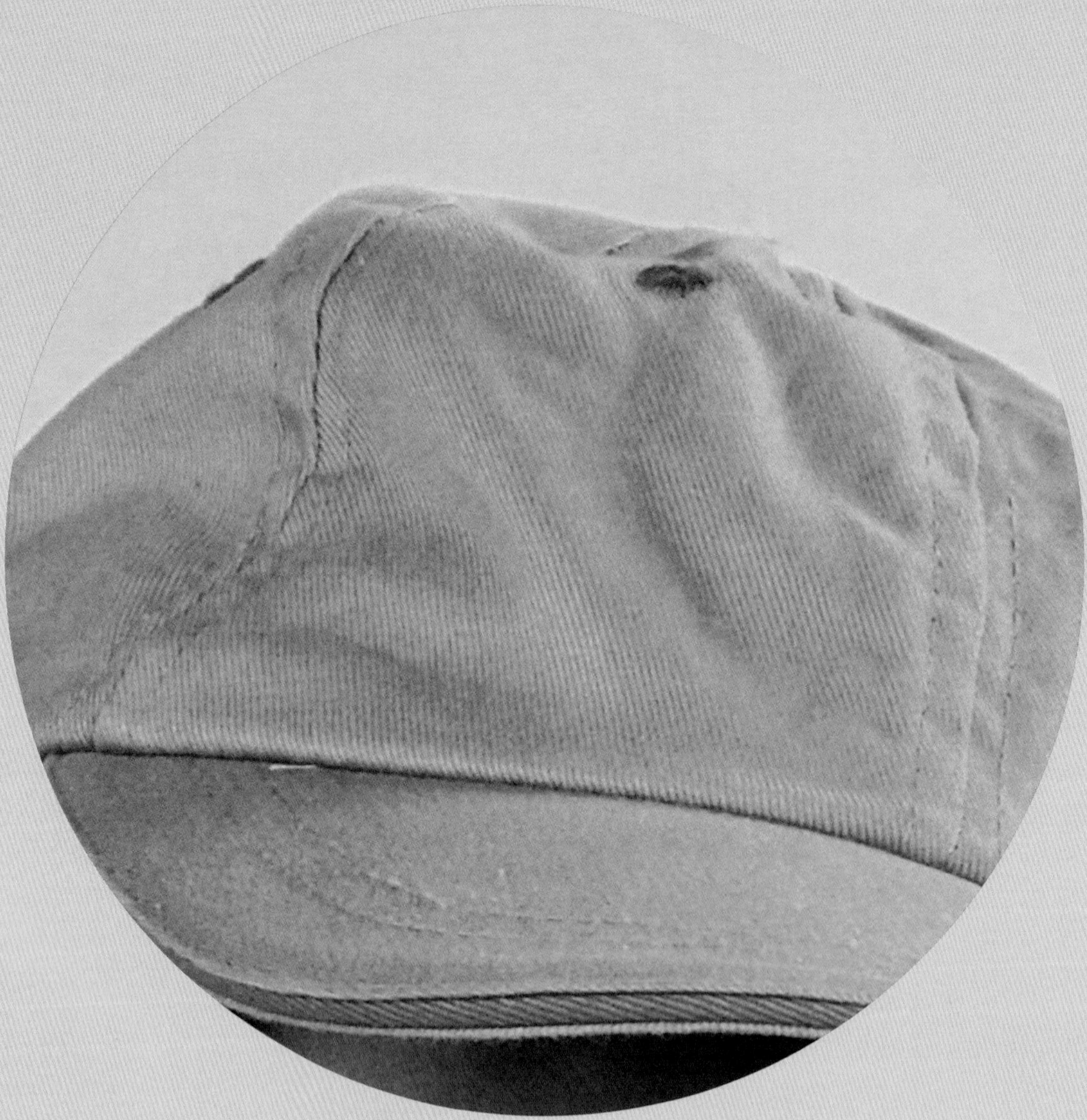

Is it a cap?

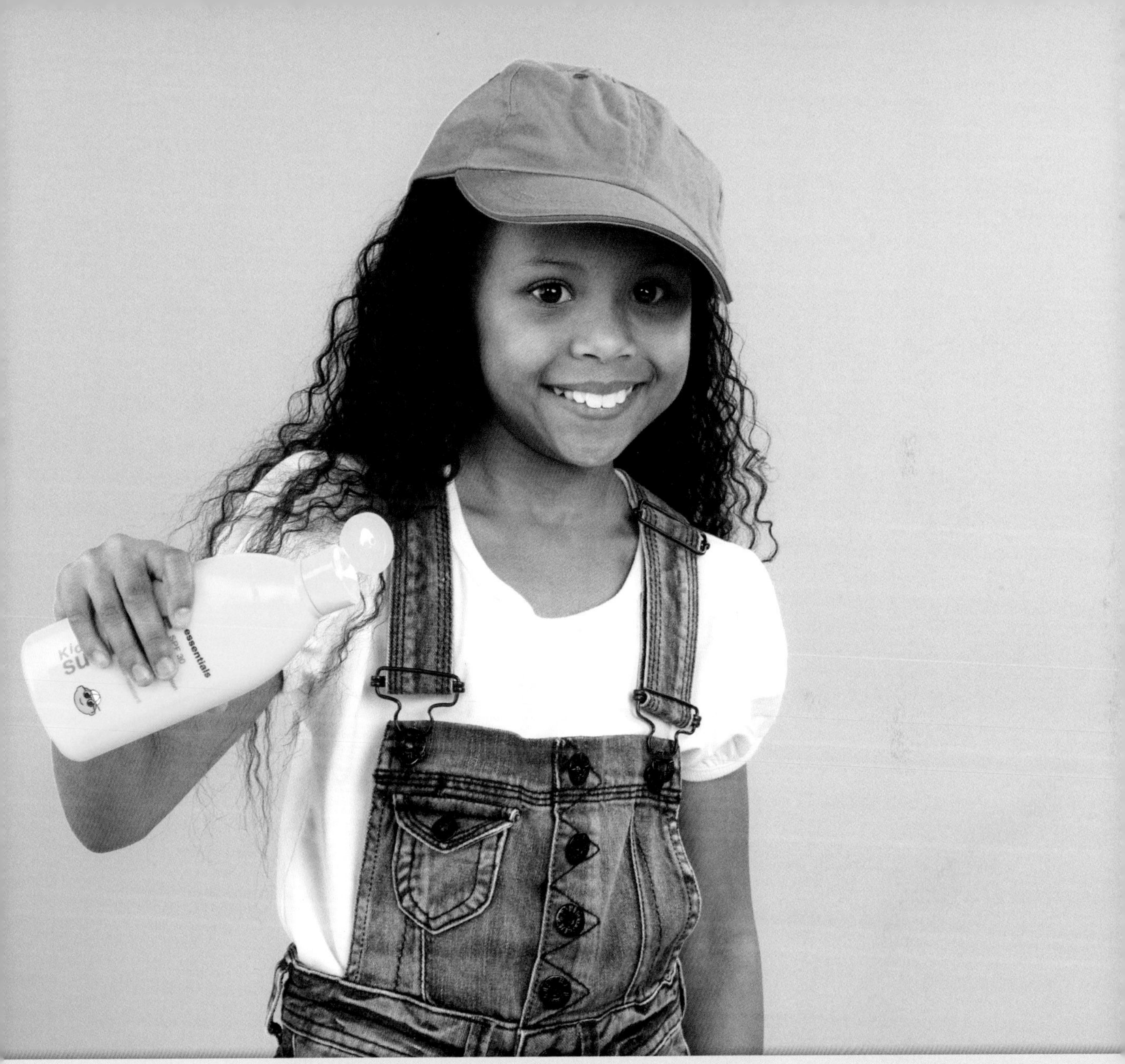

It is Kim's cap!

A cap

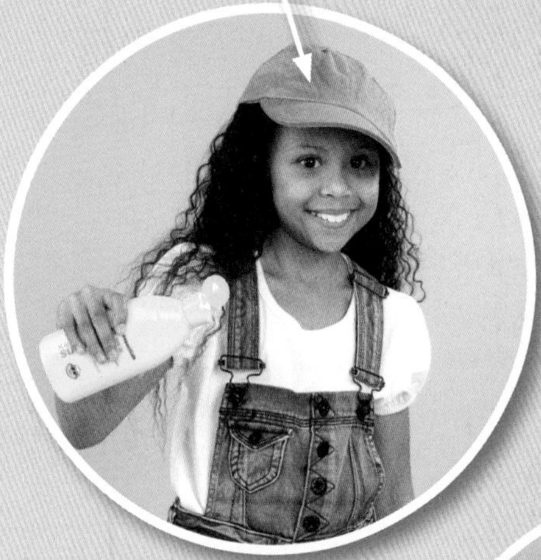

A dog

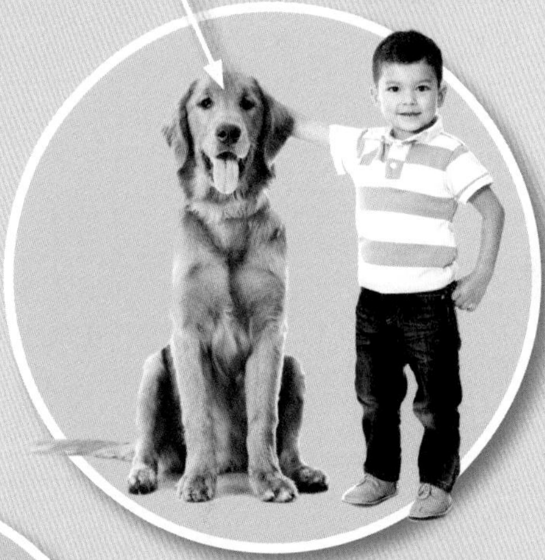

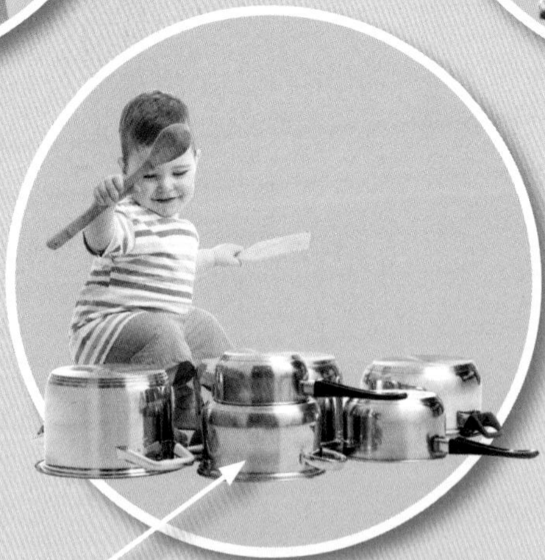

A pan